This Is the Season

by Anita B. Williams

FarMor Publishing Company
Orlando, FL

Honey for the Soul : This Is the Season

www.honeyforthesoul.com

Published by:
FarMor Publishing Company
Reaching far more than the eyes can see
P.O. Box 585633
Orlando, FL 32858
farmorpublishing@yahoo.com

Cover Photo & Design by JahGon™, Inc.
Book Design by TCGRAPHICS

Printed in the United States

Library of Congress Control Number: 2006938235

This book is dedicated to those
who may feel it's too late to reach their destiny
and discover all that God would have them to be.

It's not too late to soar on eagles' wings!

Acknowledgments

Giving thanks to:

- My Heavenly Father for trusting me with words from His heart and for also blessing me with such a gift so I may be a blessing to others.

- The Williams family for love and support: Mom and Dad; Leroy Jr.; Joseph (you are always in my heart); Wanda; and the twins, Jessica and Jasmine, and "Lil" Bit.

- Everyone that has given me an encouraging word along the way.

- Pastor Smith and the Tangelo Baptist Church family, as well as Prophet Ricardo and Teacher Trina J. Williams of the Healing of the National Ministries of Central Florida, Inc., for showing that you believe in me by giving me the opportunity to share my poems with others.

Last, but not least, I want to thank:

- My publisher, Suzette Morgan, for walking by faith and not by sight. Your persistence paid off in a mighty way. God bless you!

- JahGon™, Inc. and crew for seeing the vision and running with it the way that you all have. You have been such a blessing to me in more ways than a million. Thank you so much, and may God forever bless you.

I want to send a very special thank you to Felicia Caldwell for helping me see the gift within. May God bless you wherever you may be!

This Is the Season

by Anita B. Williams

"Pleasant words are a
honeycomb,
Sweet to the soul. . ."
**Proverbs 16:24
(NASB)**

Honey for the Soul

This Is the Season

All in the Name of Love

Never Alone

When You Believe

He Is the Reason

From the Messianic Poetess

I find it is truly a gift from God to write poetry in the manner in which He has given it to me.

I pray that I never take it for granted and that each poem will be a blessing of healing to the sick and deliverance to those in bondage.

I also pray that those who feel they are not free for one reason or another will be set free after reading the poems that are *Honey for the Soul*™ —and at times, will be *Honey to Soothe the Soul*™.

For these poems are anointed by God alone. I am the pen and He is the writer. The poems are oracles of God. They are a reply given by God for those who are in search of their place, destiny and purpose.

Honey for the Soul™ is not just words put together to sound good or to even make you feel good for whatever reason. The poems are words of truth and love.

It is truly an honor to be the one whom God has used to deliver these words. Many write and many He will use.

However, what He gives me is just for me to write and share with all who will receive in the Name of Jesus Christ.

Anita B. Williams

"To everything
there is a season. . ."

**Ecclesiastes 3:1
(NKJV)**

This Is the Season

This Is the Season
To make things right
With God

This Is the Season
To walk into the
Things of God

This Is the Season
To be all you are
Supposed to be

This Is the Season
To stop running away
And run to

Stop seeking the things
Of this world to
Give you peace
God's peace will
Surpass all understanding

Stop seeking the world's
Kind of joy
God's joy will
Give you strength

Stop seeking the world's
Kind of wisdom
God's wisdom will
Bring honor to you

This Is the Season
For you to be blessed

Soaring

Always remember it doesn't matter
If you have someone by your side
To soar with you to heights unknown
Because spiritually you do have
Someone soaring with you
And that someone is God

". . .how I bore you
on eagles' wings. . ."
Exodus 19:4
(NASB)

He is the reason you are free
So never be discouraged
When you feel lonely
On your quest to higher heights
For you are never alone on this journey
Nor are you alone when you are above the clouds

For every step and with every flight
God is with you always
Don't ever go back because of loneliness
Keep going forward and you will find
God has someone for you who is also
Soaring to heights unknown

Just keep soaring
Keep believing
Keep searching
Keep hoping in the things of God
You will find you're upon

Eagles' Wings

Soaring on Wings of Faith

Soaring on Wings of Faith
That is what it will take to reach your destiny
To be all that God would have you to be
To accomplish all that God would have you to do

Soaring on Wings of Faith
Will take you to places that others would not go
It will allow you to do things
That others would think impossible

Soaring on Wings of Faith
Will allow you to see who God really is
It will allow you to experience the things of God
That others long to, but may never,
For they doubt instead of believing

Soaring on Wings of Faith
Will open doors that would otherwise be shut
Will allow you to go to the mountaintop
And swoop down to valleys low
It will allow you to go beyond the clouds
And fly over the seas

Soaring on Wings of Faith
Will take you to the unknown
It will take you to another place in God

Soaring on Wings of Faith
Will take you wherever you want to go
In the things of God
If you will allow faith to work

Freedom

My Son
You have given so many of My children
The freedom to be all
That I would have them be

"The wise will inherit honor. . ."
Proverbs 3:35 (NASB)

Freedom
To find who I Am
In their lives

Freedom
To know that I Am with them
Even when they think not

Freedom
To explore all that I Am
And all that I have for them

Freedom
To explore the unknown without fear
But embrace it with confidence

Freedom
To soar on eagles' wings

Freedom

I Am Set Free

No longer will I ask God to
Let me be free
Now I say I am free
Free to do and accomplish
All that God would have me to

No longer am I bound by others'
Opinions or their views of who
They think I should be
Or what I should do

I Am Set Free
No longer will fear of the unknown
Keep me from my destiny
Fear will not keep me
From standing up for what I believe
That God has called me to be

Fear will not hold me back
Fear will not lead me nor guide me
Fear is no longer a part of my life

I Am Set Free
Free to soar to heights unknown to man
Heights that will show
The glory of God
That will show His power
That will show the world just how real God is

I Am Set Free
To be all that God
Has predestined me to be

"It was for freedom that Christ set us free; therefore keep standing firm and do not be subject again to a yoke of slavery."
Galatians 5:1 (NASB)

No Longer in the Box

No longer am I in the box
The box that I have allowed people to put me in
With their words of what they feel is best for me
Words that have delayed me from reaching
My destiny that God alone has set for me

No Longer in the Box
I am free to be and accomplish all that
God would have me do
Free to be the woman that I am without the fear
Of what others may think or even say—freedom

No Longer in the Box
No longer will I hold my head down
Instead, I will walk with the power that is within me
The power that allows me to do all that others said I could not
Power that God has placed within my very soul
The power that only the Anointing can bring

No Longer in the Box
No longer will the enemy hold me back
No longer will others keep me down
No longer will I allow fear to be the excuse or
The reason that I do not walk with my head up

No longer am I in the box
Fear is in the box
Doubt is in the box
Disappointment is in the box
Low self-esteem is in the box
Bondage is in the box
The past is in the box

All these things and so much more I place in the box
However, I am stepping out of the box
To walk in a new realm of where
God would have me to be

No Longer in the Box

A Light

My Precious Daughter
You have gone through
So others may see My glory
That others may know and realize
That I, the God of Israel,
Is a God of healing
Be it physical when doctors have given up
Be it mental when they say you are crazy
Be it financial when you have bills that are due
Be it spiritual when no one feels you are saved

"You, O Lord, keep my lamp burning; my God turns my darkness into light."
Psalm 18:28 (NIV)

A Light
That all can see that I Am
A God of deliverance
Be it drugs
Be it alcohol
Be it anything that puts a wall
Between Me and Mine

A Light
That others do not have to suffer
But know and understand
I Am here for them
Just as I was and still am here for you

Who Would Have Ever Thought, But God Knew

Who Would Have Ever Thought, But God Knew
Look at me serving God
I remember when, well
I won't go there
No I won't

I never thought I would be
Right here at this moment
Serving God and using the gifts
He gave me to win souls for Christ
But I am and so can you

There is something inside of you
Waiting to be birth
I know you're thinking,
I've made many mistakes
And my past is truly not the best

But I'm here to tell you
That God will wipe it all away
And give you a new start
In the right direction

Don't worry about what
Those you know will say
Because when they try
To remind you of your past
God will bring the future

And all they will be able to say is
Who would have ever thought
But God knew all along
That you were destined for greatness

Do Not Stand in My Way

Why must you put down everything I do
Why won't you allow me to be me
Why must I be something I am not
When I am around you

Why are you so afraid of the person
That God has called me to be
Don't you understand that it's not for me but
For someone who stands in need of a savior

No, I am not the Savior, but becoming
All that God would have me to be
Will allow that person to see
God through me

It will allow them to realize
That God loves them in spite of the many
Mistakes and the wrong turns they have made
On this journey to finding God and themselves

The only way any of us
Can find who we are
Is through Jesus Christ
And Him alone

What you do not understand about me
Look to God to give you the answer
All I ask is that you please do not stand in my way
Nor pass on your negative spirit

If you are not for the vision that God has given me
Then get out of my way
So I may accomplish all
That He has me to do

See I am trying to be nice and not rude
I am trying to explain to you
That I will no longer settle
For what the world says is the best
However, I will go for what God has for me
I know that it is more than the best

I do not mean to leave you behind
But if leaving you will get me to my destiny
Then I must, nothing personal
It's all about my Father's business

Do Not Stand in My Way
I am going somewhere
I will become what God alone
Has called me to be

I have a purpose
I have a destiny
I have a reason to live
I have a future to reach
I have someone who is waiting on me
To bring them a word from God

Do Not Stand in My Way

I Know What I'm Doing

Look, I know what I told you
And yes, it sounds crazy
But you must trust Me

I know where you are
And what you are in need of
Trust Me, I will provide

Look, I realize there are some
That are giving you strange looks
Because they feel you are
Wasting your life away

I hear the questions they ask you and I know
You're not quite sure what to say
Because if you told them what I said
They would not believe you

Trust Me, even when what they say
Will cause you to question
What I Am doing

Trust Me, I have you right
Where I want you
I'm using you so
Everyone will see Me

I realize this isn't easy
But this time in your life
Is in My Master Plan
I'm setting you up for greatness

Yeah, I know it's different but understand
I wouldn't have you on this journey
If I didn't think you would not go all the way

Trust Me,
I Know What I'm Doing

Finally

You have been waiting all your life
For a moment like this and still
You question if it is real or not
You wonder if you should pursue or
Hold back another day or even another year

Finally, the dream that God gave you
Some time ago is coming together
The prayer you have been praying
Is now being answered, yet you still hesitate
To walk into your destiny
The vision you had just a month ago
Is now unfolding before your very eyes
Yet, you keep wondering if you are even ready
For this moment in your life

Finally, everything is coming together
Why then are you so afraid to consume
What God alone is giving you
The door is open and the position is yours for the taking
Answer these questions
What do you think would happen
If you passed this moment by
How long do you think it would be
Before another moment like this comes again

Finally, your moment has arrived and you
Stand there in fear of the unknown
Embrace the moment and
Let God take care of the rest
For He alone brought you this far
He will take you the rest of the way
Just trust in Him

Finally, is here
What are you going to do
Whatever you do, don't let fear be the reason
You think about walking away

Finally, it is your season
It is your time to walk into your destiny
No, it is your time to become your destiny

Finally

Know Who You Are

This is your season
Do not be afraid
To walk in the calling
That I, your God,
Has placed upon you

If you were not ready
You would not be here
At this moment in time

Walk with the boldness
That I have placed within you
Walk with the authority
That the death of My Son has given you

Walk with the fear of Me and not man
Walk with the knowing that I Am with you
Every step of the way
Walk with the fact that
What you do in My Name
Shall and will come to pass

You shall heal the sick in My Name
You shall set the captive free by My words
You shall do wonders in My Name
That all will see who I Am

Know Who You Are
Know who you belong to
Know and walk with the power
That is within you

> *"Arise, shine;*
> *for your light*
> *has come,*
> *And the glory*
> *of the Lord has*
> *risen upon*
> *you."*
> **Isaiah 60:1**
> **(NASB)**

"For God so loved the world that
He gave His only begotten Son,
that whoever believes in Him
should not perish but have
everlasting life."

**John 3:16
(NKJV)**

All in the Name of Love

All in the Name of Love
Some accept the abuse they receive
By the hands of another
You ask them why
They say it is just their way of showing love
They do not mean to hurt me

We make mistakes and some bad decisions
Out of love for another, so we say
We will even make ourselves
Look foolish for love
And the price of all of this
Is a broken heart one way or another

All in the Name of Love
You bend over backwards for someone
Who has no love for you at all
You think if you show them love
That it will help them change their mind about you
Change their heart about falling in love
However, nothing you do will ever make them truly see
What beauty they would find inside of you

What are you willing to do for love
What price are you willing to pay for love
Be careful what you do in the name of love
Moreover, what you say in the name of love

Truly, everything we do and say
Has nothing to do with love at all
It's just, a lot of times, we see what we want
And we are willing to do what it takes to obtain it

No matter how good or bad the action itself may be
No matter who gets hurt in the process of obtaining
The affection of the one we are desiring
Just as long as we get what we want

There are only two people I know
Who have done all that they have for others
In the name of love
God Almighty gave up His only begotten Son
Because of His love for a dying world
He did that all in the name of love

Jesus Christ was willing
To give up His seat next to His Father
To walk among men who mocked Him
And gave Him a crown of thorns

Jesus was wounded for our transgressions
He was bruised for our iniquities
The chastisement of our peace was upon Him
He was willing to be whipped
So that by the stripes on His back
We were healed

Understand that He took that beating not so
By chance we can be healed
Or if it be in His will
But by His stripes we were healed
So in God's mind we are not sick
But in perfect health

All this was truly done in the name of love
We could never come close to what
God and Jesus Christ have done for us
So that we may have life everlasting
And peace in every area of our lives

Jesus paid it
All in the Name of Love

Wanting Love

I have been down this road so many times
And each time I have been wrong
I am down this road of 'This is the One Blvd'
Again, I think I know for sure
I think I have a lock on it, to only feel
I must be out of my mind

I cannot be hearing from God
I go to Him for answers asking
Lord is this you or me
Things happen to make me feel and think
This is God giving me a sign that
I am on key about what I am feeling
As well as thinking in my head

Then something happens to show me
That I am wrong again
This time I feel like maybe
I am never to get married
Maybe me wanting to is just that
Me wanting it and not God desiring it for me

What am I to do
Who can I talk to that will help me to understand
God please give me peace of mind because
At this very moment I have none

You see the one I think it is
Would truly be beyond anyone I could ever
Ask you for in a million years
However, when I see where I am and what I have
It is like, What would this man see in me
What could I give to him

Then I say, Why not me
God can make anyone His
Then again it would be His choice
I ask for favor in his eyes but
Only God knows the outcome of it all

Wanting to be in love
Wanting to share love with another
Hurts so bad because you want it so bad
It's like you are the only one in this world
That sees love being
The most wonderful thing in the world

I must not be of this world to want
To be with my husband so badly
I must not be of this world to want
To be in love so badly

I must not be of this world to think
That there is still hope in marriage
I must not be a child of God to think
That He would want me to be a wife

I must not be of this world
Because this is what I want
To be married
To be in love
To be with my husband

I must not be of this world
Because I believe that
I am a child of God and
He does want this for me

Your Love

Your love is everything
I have been hoping and praying for
There is nothing I can compare it to
For even if I tried, it would not capture
The true essence of your love

Your love is the sunshine on my brightest day
It is the moonlight on my darkest night
It is the rainbow after the rain
Letting me know that your love is still there
For me to harbor in my heart and soul

Your love is freedom from the bondage of past loves
Which in reality, was not love at all
You have captured a part of me
That I never knew was truly there
Yes in my mind it was just a thought
But you came along and gave it life

Your love is a reflection of God's love for me
Your love reminds me that
He truly does hear and answer prayers
He could have given your love to another
Yet, He placed it within your heart to share with me
He gave me a gift when He gave me your love

Your love, many long to have it in their lives
Some would want to control it instead of
Allowing your love to be free to explore
All that God would allow it to be

Your love cannot be bought with silver or gold
Nor priceless diamonds of any kind
Your love can only be gained
By the love of God

Your love is beyond this world
But I am glad
That I was not beyond receiving
Your Love

"Set me as a seal upon your heart, As a seal upon your arm; For love is as strong as death. . ."
Song of Solomon 8:6 (NKJV)

20

Just Love

Just Love
When God has blessed you
With someone special
Just love them for who they are

For if they weren't someone greater
God would not have allowed
Your paths to cross just when
You were ready to give up on love

Just Love
Enjoy the moment you have with them because
We don't know what tomorrow may bring
Don't waste time on foolish things
Things that have no reason nor purpose

And should there come a moment
When there is confusion
Don't let the sun set without seeking understanding
But most of all peace

Just Love
Don't let fear keep you from feeling
The true beauty and goodness
That love brings

Just Love
Because it's something special
Something that everyone longs to feel
So if you have someone to love
Don't hold on too tight
And don't push them away
With doubt and fear

Just Love
And know in your heart that
God loves you so much
He gave you a gift
Someone to love and
Someone to love you back

Just Love

I Love You

Words cannot begin to express My love
That I have for you My child
But if you would just for a moment
Leave the cares of the world behind
Your wants and desires
Your hopes and dreams
Your worries and fears
Just leave them with Me

Now close your eyes
And worship Me in spirit and in truth
As you worship, I will impart in you
All that I Am and all that
I desire for you to be

Worship Me and feel My love for you
Embrace My peace
Embrace My joy
Embrace My wisdom
Embrace My strength
Embrace all of Me, not some of Me

As you embrace Me now you will find
Just how much I love you
Just how real My love is for you
Just allow Me to love you
As you worship Me

I love moments like these
For they are so precious to Me

I Love You

Finding Someone

When you find someone to love
Do not be afraid to open your heart
To receive their love when you know
That love is true

Look into their heart and
God will allow you to see
All you need to see
He will show you
The beauty of that person
And the gifts they behold
For the gifts within are priceless

To have someone to love
Moreover, they love you back
For all the right reasons
Is truly a gift from Thee above
Never take it for granted

Always thank God above
For that special someone
For many seek to find a love
To call their own and seemly never do

When you find someone to love and
God is the reason you have found
That someone, it's more than
You could ever imagine

To Love

To love is something we all want
To feel from another
Something we want
To give to another

To love will make you feel
A part of something meaningful
There's nothing like being in love with someone
Who loves you with the same intensity

To love is an awesome feeling
You can love so deep
Until it takes your breath away

You can love so hard
Until the very thing blinds you to the point
Where you can see no wrong in that person
To the point where you cannot hear what God
May be trying to tell you about that someone

To love is wonderful and painful, all in one
Yet, we still long for
We remain in search of
We hope for that one to love
We pray this is the one
We cry every night
We feel so alone when we
Are not a part of someone

No one really knows the pain
Of not having that one you can spend
The rest of your life with
The one you grow in the Lord with
The one that no other will replace
The one that knows you like no other
The one you need but do not want
To admit to them or anyone else
That you need them

To love is all anyone really wants in this life
To love and to be loved
When you really stop to think about it
That is all God wants—to love us
He wants to shower us with love unspeakable

He wants us to know of
His mighty love
His precious love
He wants us to come
To the realization of His love

For when we do
We then can give love
We then can receive love
But most of all
We will not feel lonely anymore

To Love

God's Love Will Fill This Place

We oftentimes underestimate God's love for us
We think that He doesn't love us
Which in fact is not the case at all
His love for us is more than we could ever
Come to understand in this lifetime

We should have received a clue when
He sent His only begotten Son to die for us
But still that is not enough for us
To see His love for us, ask yourself this
Would you give up your only child
To die for just one person that you didn't know

However, God did it for many and all He knew
He already knew that we would make our mistakes
He knew that many of us
Wouldn't get it right the first 100 times
Yet, He was still willing to send His only Son
To die for me and you

God's Love Will Fill This Place
His love will carry you to the mountaintop
His love will see you through the worst of storms
It will guide you through the night
It will lead you to the path
He would have you to be on
His love is stronger than any wind
His love is deeper than any ocean
His love is wider than any sea

God's Love Will Fill This Place
It will heal a broken heart of all past hurts
No matter where or who the pain came from
His love will fill your heart up to love again
His love will change a house into a home
A church into a sanctuary of praise

God's Love Will Fill This Place
It will make a gray sky blue and
The sun shine in the midst of the storm
His love will take you to heights unknown

God's love will make you something that others
Thought you could never become
God's love will give you favor in the eyes of those
Who would otherwise use you
God's love will bring you to a place where you
Thought you would never find love

God's Love Will Fill This Place
His love will give you hope for your future
When you think there is no hope
His love will give you the strength to move on
When you would rather give up on it all

His love will keep you
When others would have fallen
He will hold you up

God's Love Will Fill This Place

In the Secret Garden of Love

In the Secret Garden of Love
The white rose is the pureness of
Our love that is of God
The red rose is the
Depth of our love that
Is within our very soul

In the Secret Garden of Love
We learn of each other's
Deep pain and sorrow
We learn how to know
Each other's thoughts without speaking
We learn how to feel each other's pain
To share each other's joy

In the Secret Garden of Love
We learn that God gave us
This love for one another
It is beyond what we could have
Ever imagined love to be

In the Secret Garden of Love
We've become one
Sharing in the most tender moments
That two people in love could share
For God has shown us the meaning
And the beauty of real love

In the Secret Garden of Love
Is where our love for one another
Began hand in hand

God bless you both
Now and Forever

Love Can Overcome

Lord, I know that love is a wonderful thing
Because You showed us
When You gave Your only begotten Son
So that we may have everlasting life

Love is stronger than anything
We could ever image in this lifetime
Love, true love that is,
Can change wrong to right

It can bring peace in the midst of a storm
No matter how bad the storm
True love can and will overcome
Evil, hurt, pain and disappointment

Lord, I know all this but tell me
Why does it hurt so bad
To love someone the way You love us
To love deeply to only be made a fool of
It seems Lord, You want all Your children
To experience true love from You
As well as from others

Lord, how do still love us
When we hurt You with our sins
And the words we say
When we reject You,
When all You want to do is
Help us go through the storm

How do You keep on loving
When we keep letting You down
You're an awesome God
But to love that way here on earth
You pay a price

But then again, we could never really pay the price
The way Your Son did when He died on Calvary
Your love gets us through when our hearts
Have been broken in such a way

True Love Can Overcome

Love Is Power

Love is such an awesome feeling
Everyone wants to feel it
Everyone wants to know of it
Everyone wants to be a part of it
In one way or another

Yet, so many of us are afraid to embrace
One of the many things that God is
We wonder how long will it be
Before love finds its way toward our hearts

You look around and you see it
Almost everywhere you go
Love could be right in front of you but
You let fear of what happened in the past
Keep you from feeling true love from someone
Who wants to give it to you from their heart and soul

You feel no one could love you so deep
However, God is showing you that
First, He loves that deep
Second, He loves through another
Embrace what you know to be true

Love Is Power
Love alone can change the heart of a cold person
To someone who loves so deeply
Love can be the difference
Between life or death
This is to be so
For God so loved the world
That He sent His only begotten Son
So that we may have everlasting life
Jesus loved us as well
For He was willing
To give up His life for our lives

Love Is Power
When you are in God

Love Is Not Enough,
But Yet, It Was Enough for God

It's funny that in the world today
Love is not enough
It's not enough for two people
To spend their lives together

For some you must have this or that
And if two people do come together
To become husband and wife
And all they really have is love
They are looked upon as if what they've done
By becoming one is a sin

Love Is Not Enough, But Yet, It Was Enough for God
He loved us so much that He sent
His only begotten Son to die
So we may be a part of His family
And have life everlasting

Love was enough for Jesus
To take the stripes on His back
For by those stripes
We are healed from every sickness

Love was enough for Jesus
To shed His blood from
The crown of His head
To the sole of His feet

Because of His blood
We are delivered
From every attack that the devil
Tries to bring our way

Love was enough for Jesus
To leave His place
At the right hand of God Almighty
To walk this earth and to die on a cross
For us whom He did not know

But Yet, Love Is Still Not Enough

Finding Love

Searching here and there
Trying to find a place where you belong
Trying to find someone to love you
And just when you think you did
Here comes the hurt and
The tears that won't end
As well as the disappointment
But in spite of
You won't stop looking for love

Then one day out of nowhere
Love finds you
You think to yourself
This is too good to be true
He couldn't love me, it's too soon

So you ask the question
How do I know Your love is true
Because I died for you
What do You mean You died for me?

You see these nail-scarred hands
You see these nail-scarred feet
These are the results of
What happened on Calvary

I hung on a cross and
I took on your sins
Your sickness, which by
The stripes on My back
You are healed

"Therefore if there is any consolation in Christ, if any comfort of love, if any fellowship of the Spirit, if any affection and mercy, fulfill my joy by being like-minded, having the same love. . ."
Philippians 2:1–2 (NKJV)

I took on your pain
Your suffering
The generational curse
Your broken heart
And so much more

But not only by My wounds
Shall you know My love is real
You see I Am God's only begotten Son

My Father loves you so much
He gave Me up
So you could have life everlasting
I was willing so My Father's will
Could be done

Who do you know
Would be willing to die for you?

At last,
Finding love, true love
At last, I know I'm loved
At last, I know I belong

At Last

You pray and dream of that special person
Coming into your life
That one person who you can share all that you are with
The one that you can have a future with

At Last
Many will never know the joy
Of having that special person
To know what it is to be loved
For all the right reasons

It's not because of your bank account
It's not because of the house you live in
It's not because of the car you drive
Nor is it because of the degree you have

At Last
To have someone in your life that loves you
Because of who you are on the inside
Because you bring the best of who they are out

Because you both know that no matter
How bad things may get
You both realize and know that
You will be there in the end for each other
As well as when you are going through

At Last
True love has come my way
A love that I can call my own
True love that is blossoming into something
That will show the love of God

At Last
My Prince has found his Princess

"... 'I will never desert you, nor will I ever forsake you.' "

**Hebrews 13:5
(NASB)**

Never Alone

There are days when
You feel on top of the world
Then there are days when
You feel like no one cares

You feel as if you don't
Have a friend in the world
When you need someone to talk to
No one is there

But my friend when
You stop and think about it
You will realize that you are
Never Alone

For God is always with you
And He feels your pain of loneliness
He is just waiting for you
To come to Him in prayer
To just talk to Him
And you will soon feel
His presence near you

So you see my friend
No matter how you may feel
Or where you are in life
You never need to worry or feel lonely
For you are
Never Alone

You Are Not Alone

Mount up on the wings of an eagle
Don't look at what is going on around you
For the most part, it's just an illusion from the devil

Now he would have you to believe
That I have left you out there
Without a wind to sail on
But know that you are not alone

I gave you the vision and
I will see it come to pass
All I ask is that you prepare My people
Teach them the Word
Give them the Word
Show them My Word

Don't worry about who will receive and who won't
That's not your concern
It's My battle and Mine alone
You stand and let Me do the rest
Prepare them for the change that is about to take place

You Are Not Alone
Trust Me, I see all and know what you are facing
That is why I have called you to the frontline

You are a soldier in My army, not man's
Trust in Me for I Am trusting you
To finish the mission at hand

You Are Not Alone

Physically No, Spiritually Yes

Physically No
You do not have anyone to call on
In the midnight hour
When it's hard to sleep and
Thoughts are running through your mind

Spiritually Yes
You have Jesus to call on
No matter the hour
He is always there waiting
To hear what's on your mind
And in your heart and soul

Physically No
You do not have that special someone
To hold you when you are feeling down
Or to comfort you with a word
That says everything will be alright

Spiritually Yes
Jesus will hold you when no one else will
He will comfort you like no other has or ever could
His words He will whisper in your ear
Are like honey that will soothe the soul

Physically No
It is like no one on this earth
Cares what you are going through
Moreover, how it is making you feel
You cry yourself to sleep
For the feeling of loneliness and rejection
Is a bit much to bear at this moment

Spiritually Yes
Jesus cares, He cares so much that
He was willing to die so you may know
Just how much God loves you
He cares, that is why He has already gone through
So your journey through this storm
Will be an easy one
If you will keep your eyes on Jesus

You are lonely but never are you alone
Jesus is with you every step of the way
He wipes away the tears
So you can see again
It does not matter the mistakes
Jesus will never reject you
He will embrace you with grace and mercy

Physically, no one can give you
The strength you need to go through
Spiritually, yes you can make it

For greater is He that is in you
Than he that is in the world

Not Alone, Yet Alone

So many are in relationships
Yet, they are alone
We ask the questions

Why do they stay
Why won't they leave
What keeps them in such a state of mind
Do they feel things will get better with time
By staying, do they feel it is the best thing

So many questions
Yet, it is so hard to find
The right answers for each one
Answers that will help us
All to understand what it is
To be with someone
Yet you are still alone

Not Alone, Yet Alone
Is it fear of being totally alone
That keeps them there
Is it fear of not being able
To make it on their own
Is it fear of the unknown future
Is it fear itself

Could love have them so blind
Could this happen to any of us
Could we find ourselves in a situation
With another that we love so
But yet being with them
Makes you feel so alone

Is it really the other one's fault
That you feel alone

Or

Could it be that you have not dealt
With issues as well unknown issues
That keep you from receiving
Love from God as well as another

Could it be you are alone within
For you have not received Jesus in your life
Alone because you haven't allowed
Your relationship with Him to grow

Ask yourself the question why
Examine yourself and search yourself
Ask God to help you find the answers
To the questions, to the truth

For He alone knows why
He alone can help you begin
To see how much He loves you
That you may begin to love yourself
So you can give love and receive love
And no longer feel alone
When you are
Not Alone

You and I

Well, Lord
It's just the way
You've wanted it
You finally have me
All to Yourself
In more ways than one

But I must admit
This is not easy
There are moments
I feel so alone like
Never before in my life
Even in a house with family
I still feel alone

There are even times
I long for the phone to ring
Hoping it's someone
Who wants to talk with me
I even want to pick up the phone
And call someone but
My heart won't let me
Even though I'm feeling lonely

So it's You and I
If this is where I'm to be
Then so be it
I know this journey
I'm on with You
I'm to learn and prepare
For my purpose

The first thing is
To realize I'm not alone
And to trust that this journey I'm on
Will put me where
I need to be

You and I

"Therefore, as the elect of God, holy and beloved, put on tender mercies, kindness, humility, meekness, long-suffering."
Colossians 3:12 (NKJV)

I Am Here

I Am Here
I Am not far, not far at all
I Am with you every step of the way
When you lay down at night
When you rise to another day

I Am Here
When you sit and think about
All that is going on around and about you
When you feel no one will understand

I Am Here
To embrace you with loving arms
To hold you with warmth beyond compare
To place you near My heart to feel
Just how real I Am

I Am Here

Have I Not Been There?

Have I Not Been There
When you needed Me the most
When your back was against the wall
And the only way out was to call on My Name

When the sky was gray
And the rain, it fell so hard
That it felt like rocks
Hitting against your very skin

Have I Not Been There
When family has walked away
As if they could care less
If you made it out of the storm or not

When the rent was due and
You had no money in the bank
When you did not have a paycheck with your name on it
When all you could do was pray and again call on My Name

Have I Not Been There
When you felt like giving up on everything, even life itself
When you thought your dream was just that, a dream
A dream with no future of any kind

Have I Not Been There
When your body was consumed with pain that not even
The pain medication the doctor gave you worked
When you were so sick that the doctors had given up
Even then, you called on My Name

Each time you had a storm raging all around you
I was there
Each time you called out My Name from your heart
I was there
The question I want you to answer for Me is
When haven't I been there?

Bond

You don't always understand
The bond you may have with another
There are times when you feel
If I could just break away

But when you try
The bond becomes tighter
So you pray and you ask God
To set you free

God responds but not
In the way you would think
You don't understand why

God says, I need you
To stand in the gap
For I have imparted in you
Something they need to get through this storm

I've bonded you together
Trust Me to work out the difficult parts
You will find it was
Worth it all

"Greater love has no one than this, than to lay down one's life for his friends."
John 15:13 (NKJV)

A Touch

All it takes is a touch
It doesn't matter what
Was said or what wasn't
A touch from God
Can change those hurting words
To words of love
Between a husband and a wife

A Touch
Can bring a drug
Addict son or daughter
Back home to the
Warm embrace of a
Praying mother and a father
Who have longed to see
Their child one more time
To make things right again

A Touch
Can change a family
That always seems to go
In a different direction
For one reason or another
To a family that prays together
That stands on the Word together
A family that is seeking God
To do His will and walk in His path

A Touch
Is sometimes all a family needs
To unite in God

"And suddenly, a woman who had a flow of blood for twelve years came from behind and touched the hem of His garment. For she said to herself, 'If only I may touch His garment, I shall be made well.'"
Matthew 9:20-21 (NKJV)

A True Friend Is a Gift

As we travel down life's road
We are bound to meet a
Friendly face along the way

"A friend loves at all times. . ."
Proverbs 17:17 (NASB)

Sometimes the way we meet is strange
But there is always
A reason and a purpose
For it all

But one thing is for sure
It's a blessing and a gift
When you come across
A True Friend
Who will not change
With the season
But will be the same
No matter the weather

God Bless You
My Beloved Friend

I Never Want To Be Too Far Away

It has been awhile since I just sat down
And had a chat with You
I mean just You and I talking about the
Deep things of Your heart

To be real about it, I have missed those times
More than I had come to realize
And I understand as well that
I never want to be too far away from You

I need this one on one with You
For they are special to me
They mean more to me
Than words could ever really say

I know it is my own doing
That we have not spent any time together
I ask that You forgive me for letting other things
Seem more important than my time with You

Forgive me for taking for granted the special way
We share with one another
No matter what happens or don't
I never want to be too far away from You

I don't want to go without hearing You speak
The way You do to me
I want to be near and
Always hearing Your every word

For Your words are truly priceless
Your words are life in a lifeless situation
Your words are hope
Your words are peace
Your words are strength
Your words are joy
Your words are love

Your words are what keep me going
When I want to stop
It is the reason I have been feeling
Like I do not hear You
Because I haven't heard Your words in my special way
The way that some hear and others wonder how

I Never Want To Be Too Far Away
Because when I am
I feel lost and alone

Lord it feels good to be back in our favorite spot
Talking again the way we used to
There is nothing like these moments I have with You
The one moment where I get to feel
And hear Your heartbeat
This is my time and I will not give it up
For anyone or anything

I Never Want To Be Too Far Away

By Your Side Is Where I Want To Be

The pain of my past had me feeling
That love would never come my way
But God had a plan
That would allow me to have love
In a special kind of way

No longer do I have to be the one
To carry the burden
Nor do I have to be the one
To lead or guide
No longer do I have to stand alone
When the storm is raging on every side

No longer do I have to face
A battle alone or wonder if
There will be someone I can to turn to
Or even have a shoulder to cry on

No longer will I have to be afraid of the unknown
For I have someone to stand with
I have someone who is willing
To take the lead and guide me
Through the storm

God being your guide
I know that the path we travel
God is leading and guiding you

For I know that God has placed
My heart in your hands
Because He trusts you
To take care of it

By Your Side Is Where I Want To Be
No matter what
By your side is my destiny

The past is just the past
There is nothing I can do to change it
For if I could change it
I would not be where I am at this moment
And that is by your side

I have made my mistakes
I have been disappointed
I have been let down
But had I not
I would not be the woman I am today
For who I am today has placed me
By your side and that is where
I want to be

I will not let the past hang over me
Nor will I let my journeys with others
Hold me back from receiving
All that you are willing
To give and share with me

You are my true destiny

"And whatever things you
ask in prayer, believing,
you will receive."

**Matthew 21:22
(NKJV)**

When You Believe

Jesus said to him
'If you can believe
All things are possible
To him who believes'

Just believe and it will be
All God wants us to do is believe
That what He says will happen
We can believe in the negative things
To happen in our lives a whole lot quicker
Than we will the things of God

We question it
We will analyze it
We will doubt it
We will go back and forth
Before we believe
Why?

Why is it so hard to believe
That God will come through
Why do we have to figure it out
Before we give the situation over to God
God has an answer to everything in His Word

If you need a healing
He has the scriptures you can stand on
He has proof that He will heal
If you just read
You will find many testimonies of people
Who have been healed

If you need deliverance,
He again has scriptures you can stand on
Again, He has proof of His work
All you have to do is read
And you will find the proof
With the help of the Holy Spirit
He will break it down
That you may see for yourself
His power just by reading

You can find what you need in His Word
However, if you do not believe in His words
It will prove to be nothing to you and
You will wonder why nothing is changing in your life
You see, faith without works is dead
But when you believe
You are putting your faith to work

When you walk with God
You walk by faith and not by sight

For God will only tell in part
There will be times
When it seems like God is not moving
But know that He is no matter what
You must believe

Understand that "without faith
It is impossible to please Him,
For he who comes to God
Must believe that He is. . ."
Hebrews 11:6 (NKJV)

Do Not Give Up!

The battle is on
The battle of tradition vs. change
I know My son
That you are up against those
Who think they run My house
They think they have the final say
On what goes on in My house

But remember who made
The heavens and the earth
Remember I Am the Beginning and the End
As well as the In Between

Listen but do not take heed
Do not allow their words to conform you
But allow it to draw you
Evermore closer to Me

Do Not Give Up!
I know even now
As you read My words
You want to walk away

You would rather just disappear
If, but for a moment,
Just enough time to allow yourself
To breathe again

They think they are in control
But they will see and realize
That My will, will be done
Whether they choose to walk with you or not

Some I may have to remove in order
For the vision to come to pass
But understand My son
I called you to be where you are

I have shaped, made and molded you, not men
Even through this struggle
I Am preparing you
For an even much more greater task

Do Not Give Up!
Stand and watch Me fight
This battle for you
Stay before Me so that
I may impart My strength in you
For when you are weak
I Am made strong

No, not all see nor do they understand
However, know that tradition will die
For I will do a new thing to reach the lost
Too many are looking to the world
To help them out of their hurt and bondage

I see and hear what others don't
And it grieves Me
It will take something
Different to reach them

Do not worry nor concern yourself
With how many will join you
Just keep on moving toward the vision
I will place those in your life
Who will see the vision and run with it

Do Not Give Up!
Always remember that I Am with you
It is by My grace
That you are still standing

Know Your Worth

Know Your Worth
Do not settle for just anything or anyone
Why should you when you are My child
I Am That I Am

I Am Alpha and Omega
The first and the last
There is truly none like Me
So why settle for less than the best

Know Your Worth
Do not let what others say about you
Determine what you are worth
For all will not see the many treasures that
I, alone, have placed within your very being

Do not let the attitude
That others may have toward you
Keep you from seeing all that I see in you
Do not let it blind you or hold you back
From the love that I have for you
Never let what they do
Build a wall between Me and you

Know Your Worth
Yes, I know and realize that
You long for that love from another
The kind of love that shows how important
You are, as well as how special

Allow Me if you will
To send that special someone your way
I am still working on him
So he will be whole
When he steps to you, My daughter,

". . .for he who touches you touches the apple of His eye." **Zechariah 2:8 (NKJV)**

Know Your Worth
You are worth more than rubies
And much more than diamonds
You are truly priceless and
When the one that I have
Comes your way
He will see just how priceless you are

He will see you in another light and run with it
He will not be afraid of the woman you have become
For he knows that he is the man for you
For I have prepared him to be

Know Your Worth
Walk in it
Talk it
Show it
Embrace it
Live it

Do not allow anything or anyone to stop you
Stand as the Queen that you are
For your King awaits you with a heart
Full of love and peace
Love and peace that I placed within him
Just for you

Know Your Worth

A Change Is Coming

A Change Is Coming
Right now you feel
As if God has forgotten you
Because nothing around you is changing

The tears that fall from your eyes
In the middle of the night
Are still tears of pain
It's not the joy
That you long to feel and
Need so much at this time

You don't want a bandage
Because that will only last for a moment
Before you need another

You want a healing
You want a deliverance
You want the winds to bring a change
That will bless you
Like never before in your life

A Change Is Coming
A new journey

A Change Is Coming
One that will give you hope
In your darkest moment
One that will allow you
To soar a little higher
Like the eagle

A Change Is Coming
Because God is moving
Heaven and earth for you

When It Happens

When It Happens
There will be no words that could come close
To explaining the joy you feel
Of having a prayer answered and
A dream come true

Words could never really say
What it is like to walk in your purpose
That God alone has placed over your life
To watch it finally unfold before your very eyes

When It Happens
The world will see God's hands upon your life
They will see all that you have gone through
Was for this greater moment in your life

They will know that God can and will use whom
He has chosen to fulfill His purpose
Not according to man but to Him alone

Many would have counted you out for all the
Mistakes you have made along the way
However, God sees all that we cannot

He knows all we will not
Therefore, He alone knows and sees
What it will take for you to walk into that which
He has called you to do

When It Happens
It will be sweet to your soul
It will be joy to your heart
It will be more than you could ever dream
This moment would bring

When It Happens
What a joyous day it will be

Your Breakthrough Is Tailor-Made Just for You

"Would not God find this out? For He knows the secrets of the heart."
Psalm 44:21 (NASB)

Everybody's breakthrough is different
No one person is the same
Not all will understand or even see
How that could truly be

Your breakthrough may come through spiritual dance
Whereas someone else's breakthrough will come
Through their shout unto the heavens
My breakthrough may come through my tears
But all will come through our praise unto God Almighty

Your Breakthrough Is Tailor-Made Just for You
Do not let anyone make you feel that you must be strong
At all times as you go through your storm
Whatever that storm may be
Know that in your weakest moment
You can still find strength to take you to the next step
That moment of weakest may be what you need
At that time and moment
Only God knows what will help you
Get to the next level in Him

Just understand that in that moment
Where you find yourself not able to go on
Don't let it keep you there
Do what you must to get back on the right track
If you must dance in the spirit then dance
If you must get your shout on then shout
If you must speak in tongues then speak
If you must cry then cry

If you find yourself not able to do anything at all
Then just call on the Name of Jesus
For there is power in the Name of Jesus
His name is above all names
Every knee shall bow
And every tongue confess
The Mighty Name of Jesus
There is just something about that Name Jesus

Your Breakthrough Is Tailor-Made Just for You

"... 'I AM WHO

I AM'..."

**Exodus 3:14
(NASB)**

He Is the Reason

He Is the Reason
Yes, the doctor gave you the diagnosis of the illness
However, God is the reason you are still here
Where the doctor is confused about
Why this is happening and why that is happening
God isn't confused, He has just what you need to be healed
He knew that this moment in your life would be

He is the reason you are healed
For by the stripes of Jesus you are whole again
He is the reason you woke up this morning in your right mind
That you can get up out of bed and walk
You can pick up the phone and talk
You can give Him praise
Even when your body is tired
Your spirit, man, is strong
You can wave your hands in the air and say
Thank you, Jesus

He is the reason when the devil wants to hold you down
He sends His Word through others
He leads brothers and sisters to pray and
Stand in the gap on your behalf
When you find it hard to pray and battle for yourself
God has assigned certain warriors to you

Do not hold it in and do not hold your head down
Let it go and let God
Hold your head up and give Him all the praise
For He spoke and it was done
He commanded and it stood fast
He is the author and finisher of our faith

He is the reason you can and will go on
To show what God can and will do
When the enemy comes against you
He is the reason you can stand and hold your head up

He is the reason you are a testimony
Let the weak say I AM STRONG

Immanuel, God With Us

Born to a virgin, son of a carpenter
Was wrapped in swaddling cloths
And laid in a manger
For there was no room in the inn

Placed on His shoulder even at birth
Were the sins of the world
His gift is that He would die for us
That we may have life everlasting

Immanuel
A name above all names
A name that can be called on
No matter where you are
A name that no gift can compare
To its glory or strength

Immanuel
A name that will give you peace
In the midst of a storm
Joy when you have no joy
Favor among those who, otherwise,
Would pass you by
A name that will bring healing in your body
When doctors have given up

Immanuel
He will be called
Wonderful Counselor
Mighty God
Everlasting Father
Prince of Peace

Immanuel, God With Us

Joseph, Did You Know?

Joseph, Did You Know
That the baby boy
Who was born to you
Would change history

Did You Know
That He would suffer and
Endure so much pain and heartache
For those whom He did not know
Nor would ever meet

Did you even realize
That He would be betrayed
By those closest to Him
That He would be rejected
And humiliated

Did You Know
That He would be known as
King of kings and
Lord of lords
The Prince of Peace

That His Name
Would be above all names
That every knee will bow and
Every tongue will confess

Joseph, Did You Know?

Celebrating His Life

It's not about giving, receiving nor exchanging of gifts
It's not about the decorations we put up
Around our homes or in the stores

Celebrating His Life
Is about the night that He was born
That night changed everything
Around the world and in our lives

For if we were to stop and think about it
If Jesus were not born
We would not be
Entitled to everlasting life

We would not be able to say
By His stripes we are healed
So believe for a healing

We would not be delivered from all the
Bondage that the devil tries
To put upon us each and every day
For by the shedding of His blood
We are set free

Celebrating His Life
Is an honor and a privilege
As children of the living God
So many do not recognize His birth
For they get caught up in the season
Instead of the reason for the season
Jesus Christ

Celebrating His Life
Is the best gift, is it not?

Some Are Without

In your mind you may be asking
What does this statement mean
Some Are Without
During this holiday season
So many are sitting alone for whatever reason

Not all choose to be this way
However, that's the way it is for them
Some do not have jobs
Therefore, they have little or no money
To buy anything for themselves
Let alone for their families

Some Are Without
Love, peace, joy, happiness and Jesus
We take for granted the things
That most of us get every day
One way or another
We cannot even begin to understand
Those who are without
How they are feeling during this time of the year

It's not just those without a job
There are those who have jobs and a lot of money
Yet, they are still without the things that
Jesus came to this earth to give
Each and every one of us

We can go through without giving thought
Of the next person and I guess
Because of the way the world is,
It is no wonder

Still, Some Are Without
What can we, as children of God, do
To make seasons like these
So special for them as they are for us
What can we do to make every day
A day worth moving on for
A day that will give them hope
To even want to see tomorrow

Some Are Without
But if you are reading this
Maybe you as well
Are without something that you feel
Will make things right in your life
The only answer I have to give is
Jesus is the only one
Who can change our lives

It does not matter where you have been
It does not matter where you are now
It does not matter what stage you are in
At this time in life or the season

It does not matter what you have or do not have
For no one will ever out give God Almighty
Nor can you buy your way into His heart
We all must come to the realization
That God is the 'without'
That is needed in our lives

Some need to accept Him in
Others need to come back
You may be running
You need to stop and embrace your calling
We all need a closer walk with thee
No matter where you are
Who you are or where you think you want to go

We need to stop being without God in our lives
We need to take the time out and
Hear the sound of His mighty heartbeat
With the love He has, feels and longs to give
To all whom is willing to receive

Some Are Without
However, none of us has to be

A Newness

A New Year is now upon us
With a chance to start a new path
One that will allow us to use the past
As a guide but not to repeat that
Which has already happened

A chance for us to come closer
To fulfilling our purpose that
God has planned for our lives

We must not be afraid
Neither of the unknown nor the mistake
That we may make along the way
The mistake will let us know of the wrong turns
And through the Holy Spirit
We will know which way is the right way

A Newness
A time of new birth, of new beginnings
Another opportunity to become all that
God would have us to be
We must walk into that which
He has called us to

For there are so many who are hurting
For one reason or another
They are looking for a life jacket called Jesus
For they know that deep down
He is the only one
Who can and will rescue them
In spite of where they have been
Or even where they are at this present time

We have been praying for this moment
This moment is now here
What will any of us do with this moment

Will we waste it away
To only realize that time is gone and
We pray for another chance of new beginnings

On the other hand, will we go for it
Not worrying about the outcomes
However, trusting God no matter what

Where will this New Year find you
What will you bring or even become
After all is said and done

God is doing a new thing
To get us all on the right track

A Newness
That we all have been waiting for

God's Gift

For unto us a child is born
Unto us a Son is given. . .
And His name will be called
Wonderful Counselor

His words will comfort you in sickness
Which will bring about a healing
Through death, which will bring joy to your heart
Through tears that will endure through the night
But the sun will shine in the morning
Through pain, for when we are weak
He is made strong

Mighty God
Will make a way out of no way
When hope seems lost
He is the ray of light
When others find excuses
He has the Master Plan
When the things of this world
Seem too much to bear
Greater is He

Everlasting Father
He will be there to wipe away the tears
That fall like rain and hold you in His arms near His heart
He will encourage you in a way that
Only a father can
He will uphold you when you are about to fall

Prince of Peace
No matter how rough the wind may blow
No matter how hard the rain may fall
No matter how dark the sky may get
He will be your peace in the midst of it all

God's Gift is everlasting
In and out of season